D1538324

Read All About
Earthly Oddities

CAVES

Patricia Armentrout

The Rourke Press, Inc.
Vero Beach, Florida 32964

PHOTO CREDITS
© Armentrout: pg. 12; © Djuna Bewley: pg. 13; © David Bunnell: Cover, pgs. 4, 6, 7, 9, 10, 16, 18, 21, 22; © James P. Rowan: pgs. 15, 19

ACKNOWLEDGMENTS
The author wishes to acknowledge David Armentrout for his contribution in writing this book.

Library of Congress Cataloging-in-Publication Data

Armentrout, Patricia, 1960-
    Caves / by Patricia Armentrout.
       p. cm. — (Earthly Oddities)
    Includes index.
    Summary: Describes the formation and different parts of caves, including the entrance zone, twilight zone, and dark zone.
    ISBN 1-57103-152-9
    1. Caves—Juvenile literature.   [1. Caves.]
I. Title II. Series: Armentrout, Patricia, 1960-   Earthly Oddities.
GB601.2.A76 1996
551.4'47—dc20   96–2894
                                                                      CIP
                                                                      AC

Printed in the USA

TABLE OF CONTENTS

CAVES AND CAVERNS

Caves are natural hollow areas in the ground. Some caves are too small for a person to crawl into. Large caves, sometimes called caverns, have hundreds of miles of passages. Over 300 miles of passages have been explored in the Mammoth Cave system in Kentucky.

Caves and caverns are home to many kinds of birds, snakes, and other animals. The most famous cave dweller is the bat. Bats fly like birds, but are actually mammals.

Some cave passages are a tight squeeze.

HOW CAVES ARE FORMED

Most caves form in a type of rock called limestone, although some are formed in **volcanic lava** (vahl KAN ik) (LAH vuh).

Caves are formed when rain or river water soaks into the limestone rock below. The water has **carbon dioxide** (KAHR bun) (dy AHK syd) in it. Water and carbon dioxide together make a mild acid.

Some caves contain underground lakes and rivers.

Cave explorers must use special equipment to get to certain areas of a cave.

The acid water drains into cracks in the limestone. As it does, it slowly dissolves the limestone; and the cracks grow larger and larger, eventually forming a cave.

STALACTITES

If you have ever been in a cave, you may have seen what looks like icicles hanging from the ceiling. These strange formations are called **stalactites** (stuh LAK TYTS). They form in the same way an icicle forms.

As water slowly drips from the ceiling of the cave, it carries small amounts of limestone with it. The water dries up and leaves some of the limestone behind.

Because this process takes thousands of years, cave visitors should be careful not to break or damage the fragile formations.

Cave explorers must be careful not to damage fragile limestone formations.

STALAGMITES

Stalagmites (stuh LAG MYTS) are similar to stalactites. Instead of growing down from the ceiling, they grow up from the floor of the cave.

As water drips from the cave ceiling and splashes to the floor, it carries small amounts of limestone with it. Over thousands of years the limestone slowly builds up, growing taller and taller.

As stalactites grow down and stalagmites grow up, they sometimes meet each other, forming a column. It can take over a 100,000 years for a column to form.

Imagine how long it has taken for this column to form.

THE ENTRANCE ZONE

The entrance zone of a cave is an area not too different from the surface outside. During the day there is plenty of light, and many types of plants grow here. **Trogloxene** (TRAHG luh zeen) is the name given to animals that live in the entrance zone. It means "cave visitor."

These cave visitors sit inside the entrance zone of a small cave.

Snakes are one of many kinds of animals that make their homes in caves.

Small animals, such as mice and snakes, make their home in the entrance zone. Birds sometimes build nests on the cave walls, which makes it easy for them to come and go as they search for food outside.

Large animals, like bears, may live in the entrance zone, too. In fact, cave explorers have found over 50,000 bear skeletons in one cave in Austria.

THE TWILIGHT ZONE

As you move farther into a cave, you enter an area that scientists call the twilight zone. Less light makes it to this area of the cave. The animals that live here are called **troglophiles** (TRAHG luh fylz), which means animals that like living in caves.

Troglophiles sleep in the cave during the day, but they leave the cave at night to find food. Spiders, crickets, owls, and bats share the twilight zone. Every night, as many as one million bats fly from Carlsbad Caverns in New Mexico in search of food.

Crickets are found in the twilight zone of a cave.

THE DARK ZONE

The dark zone of a cave is an area of total darkness. The temperature never changes. The animals that live here are called **troglobites** (TRAHG luh byts). They are true cave dwellers because they spend their entire lives inside the cave.

There are fish, worms, salamanders, and many kinds of insects in the dark zone. Most of these dwellers are completely blind. In total darkness, eyes are not very useful. Instead, most troglobites have highly developed senses of hearing, smell, taste, and touch.

A spider finds a water source while a visitor looks on.

CAVE EXPLORATION

There are thousands of caves all over the world. Probably many others have yet to be discovered.

Caves that have not been explored are called wild caves. Wild caves can be dangerous and should only be explored by experts.

Underwater caves can be explored when using the proper equipment.

Bats are probably the most famous cave residents.

Some famous caves have been turned into show caves. They are equipped with lights, stairs, and railings, making it possible for people to visit them in safety.

Maybe you will explore a cave someday. If so, visit a show cave or go with an expert who can teach you how to explore caves safely.

PEOPLE AND CAVES

Caves provide a natural home for many animals. Caves offer protection from rain, snow, and sleet. The temperature does not rise and fall inside a cave the way it does outside.

People have also used the protection of caves for the same reasons animals do. Scientists have discovered drawings on cave walls that prove humans lived there thousands of years ago.

Even today, there are places in the world where people live in caves. Some of these modern cave dwellers have even installed electric lights in their caves.

Show caves are equipped with lights and railings.

GLOSSARY

carbon dioxide (KAHR bun) (dy AHK syd) — a colorless gas in the air

stalactites (stuh LAK TYTS) — formations that hang down from cave ceilings, growing over time by dripping water and limestone

stalagmites (stuh LAG MYTS) — formations that reach up from cave floors, growing over time from dripping water and limestone

troglobites (TRAHG luh byts) — a name given to animals that live only in the dark zone of a cave

troglophiles (TRAHG luh fylz) — a name given to animals that live in the twilight zone of a cave

trogloxene (TRAHG luh zeen) — a name given to animals that live in and outside the entrance zone of a cave

volcanic lava (vahl KAN ik) (LAH vuh) — melted rock that comes from an opening in the Earth called a volcano

Exploring caves is fun but should only be done with an expert cave explorer.

INDEX